BREAD BROKEN

BREAD BROKEN
Journey through the Cross

Reflections by Bishop David Konstant

Images and accompanying text by
Sr Mary Stephen CRSS

McCRIMMONS
Great Wakering, Essex

First Published in United Kingdom in 2008 by
McCRIMMON PUBLISHING CO. LTD.
10-12 High Street, Great Wakering, Essex, SS3 0EQ, England.
Telephone: 01702-218956 Fax: 01702-216082
info@mccrimmons.com
www.mccrimmons.com

ISBN 978-085597-691-0

Cover design and layout by Nick Snode
Printed on 110gsm smooth art / 260gsm art (one-sided)
Printed by Thanet Press Ltd., Margate, Kent, UK.

CONTENTS

1	CHRIST BREAKS THE BREAD	6
2	GETHSEMANE	8
3	JESUS IS SCOURGED	10
4	JESUS IS CROWNED	12
5	JESUS IS CONDEMNED TO DEATH	14
6	JESUS TAKES UP HIS CROSS	16
7	JESUS FALLS FOR THE FIRST TIME	18
8	JESUS MEETS HIS MOTHER	20
9	SIMON OF CYRENE SHARES THE BURDEN	22
10	VERONICA WIPES HIS FACE	24
11	JESUS FALLS A SECOND TIME	26
12	JESUS MEETS SOME WOMEN OF JERUSALEM	28
13	JESUS FALLS YET AGAIN	30
14	JESUS IS STRIPPED OF HIS CLOTHES	32
15	JESUS IS NAILED TO THE CROSS	34
16	JESUS IS CRUCIFIED	36
17	JESUS IS TAKEN DOWN FROM THE CROSS	38
18	JESUS' BODY IS LAID IN THE TOMB	40
19	ON THE THIRD DAY JESUS ROSE FROM THE DEAD	42
20	BREAKING THE BREAD IN GOD'S KINGDOM	44

1   CHRIST BREAKS THE BREAD

"I start with the Breaking of the Bread,
the symbol of what is to come, only it is far more than a
symbol because that bread has become his body.
From there he sets out on a journey of his 'Passion'."

Sr Mary Stephen CRSS

If bread is to be shared
it must be broken.
Fraction does not destroy;
but enables us first to share,
so that we may be built up.

"He who eats my flesh
shall have eternal life"
says Jesus.

This is real food,
it gives life and strength,
it is food for the journey,
the journey that leads
through death to an undreamed of future.

The hands that break the bread
are strong, and sure.
As we begin our journey with the cross
may we find the strength,
and the confidence to be –
    unworried …
    untroubled …
    without fear for the future ...
trusting in your saving presence.

**Lord,
when we are broken
help us to know
that we are safe in your hands
and that we may ever grow
in confidence and hope.
Amen!**

"Foreseeing what is to come, Jesus goes to pray – to prepare himself. Overwhelmed by the horror of what is to follow, in agony he throws himself prostrate on the ground among the shadows of the olive trees.
He begs his Father to find another way. The tautness of his arms stretching out in front of him expresses the intensity of his agony."

Sr Mary Stephen CRSS

Foresight is a mixed blessing.
Forewarned is forearmed,
but the future can be frightening,
and it may well be better
if it is shown to me only gradually
so that I may grow in courage and strength,
in answer to the stress of the moment.

As Jesus glimpsed into the future
he was utterly overwhelmed
    … prostrated.
Sweat fell from him like drops of blood.
Truly this was an agony
    … of apprehension
    … of fear
    … of dread.
He was at the threshold of despair.
"How can this be?" he pleaded
knowing but only partly knowing,
fearful in the shadowland of Gethsemane.
Yet he was unbroken.

"Not my will, but yours be done!"

**Lord!
cherish me –
protect me –
strengthen me –
so that I may be better able
to bear the pains of my own suffering
– physical, mental, emotional, spiritual –
and like you be always ready, and at peace.
I pray in union with the Suffering Lord.
Amen!**

3 JESUS IS SCOURGED

"In this series I have passed over the intervening episodes and have stopped to dwell on the scourging.
Here the hands are expressing something of the pain that is happening to other parts of his body, and the dominant red colour for me expresses the intensity of his pain."

Sr Mary Stephen CRSS

Lashed to a pillar for a frightful torture –
    arms roped ... hands clamped ... flesh torn ...
His whole body –
    battered by the agony ... wrapped in pain ...
    criss-crossed by the lashes ...

Words cannot convey the exquisite horror
    of Christ's scourging.
Images hint at what imagination flees from.
Yet through both eye and tongue
we grasp something,
though we baulk at the truth,
    that this is God's own Son

At this dreadful time
Jesus's whole being is absorbed ...
    consumed ... flooded ...
by the remorselessness of it all.

Let me reflect on the need for tenderness in my life –
    towards those who are being hurt ...
    towards those responsible for their hurt ...
    towards the hard of heart ...
    towards the weak and vulnerable ...
    towards the inadequate ...
    and especially towards myself.

"Compassionate your Saviour thus cruelly treated."

Lord Jesus,
in my own agony,
great or slight as it may be,
I come to you with hope and trust,
for with you all things are possible,
and all manner of things shall be well.
Amen.

4   JESUS IS CROWNED

"He is crowned, but it is with thorns.
Again the intensity of the pain is expressed by the
vibrant red.
The thorns are too sharp to handle so they are jammed on
his head with heavy gloved hands."

Sr Mary Stephen CRSS

"Are you a king?" asked Pilate.
"I am" said Jesus.
Of course a king must have a crown,
but what a shocking one is this
to be thrust on his head –
     steel-like thorns ... jagged spikes ...
     remorseless claws ... tearing at his head.

"Hail King!" taunt the soldiers
     spitting in his face ...
     jamming on his crown ...
     laughing at their games ...
Perhaps we should not blame them,
they were only obeying orders
and, of course, this allows every excess – even torture.
Yesterday, today, for ever,
the same excuses parade themselves,
and Christ is racked again
     by sin ... by weakness ... by false love ... by fear ...

"Are you a king?" asks Pilate of Jesus,
and he acknowledges this truth.
"Crown him with many crowns", we sing.
Truly he is universal King, and Lord of all –
he rules with justice, gentleness and compassion ...
he guides through the thickets of confusion ...
he leads to fresh pastures for our refreshment ...
for his sovereignty is for ever and always.

God of love,
you have raised your Son Jesus
to be King of all creation resplendent in glory.
Open our hearts so that we may rejoice in his peace,
practise his justice, and live in his love.
Amen!

5   JESUS IS CONDEMNED TO DEATH

*"Here we begin with the traditional 'Stations of the Cross'.
This speaks for itself, I think, except perhaps to say that the
red is intended as more than his red centurion's cloak and
its reflection (the cloaks were not that long!). It speaks of
the blood he is shedding – both in the scourging and
crowning and the crucifixion to come."*

Sr Mary Stephen CRSS

The Stations of the Cross mark twelve fearful
moments on Jesus's staggering way
that would end on the hill of Calvary.
It was a pain-racked journey that began in Pilate's Palace.
Pontius Pilate had a hard choice to make –
to let Jesus go free, and risk a riot ...
to have him executed, knowing that he had done no wrong ...

We know the choice he made and how he showed it,
how he washed his hands of his duty –
his gesture has become a symbol of
cowardice ... fear ... irresponsibility ... guilt ...
But before I condemn him,
perhaps I must acknowledge
that these are my failings too.
So often in my life I fail to do what is right
because, like Pilate, I am scared of what I may be led to.

Like all my companions
I know I must cultivate certain great strengths
that will lead me to a greater maturity and fullness of being –
the readiness to forgive others (and myself) ...
the trustfulness that inspires confidence ...
the willingness to accept responsibility ...
Thus may I respond to Jesus's hopes for me.

**Remember Lord,
not just those of good will, but also those of ill will,
not just our suffering, but the fruits of this suffering –
our comradeship, loyalty, humility, courage,
generosity and greatness of heart –
which has grown out of all this.
And when they come to judgement,
let all the fruits that we have borne,
be their forgiveness. Amen.**

A prayer reputed to have been found at Ravensbruck concentration camp in Nazi Germany.

6 JESUS TAKES UP HIS CROSS

"Even though he must be stooping under the weight of the cross he looks determinedly ahead to the painful journey.
He does not shrink from it."

Sr Mary Stephen CRSS

This is the beginning of a dreadful,
frightening journey –
short in distance ... endless in anticipation and dread ...

The path is a parable of Jesus's agony –
 rough and rocky ... steep and plunging ...

The cross was his present burden,
so soon to become his scaffold.
The cross conveyed nothing but
 torture ... humiliation ... death ...

Ponder the nature of a cross –
 heavy ... an encumbrance
 awkward ... a yoke
 rough ... abrasive
No wonder he prayed to be freed,
 "Father if it be possible
 let this cup pass from me!"

But we must also remember the promises,
 "My yoke is easy, my burden light" ...   *Matthew 11:30*
 The house built on rock is secure ...   *Luke 6:48*

So the Cross has now become for us,
through his willingness to embrace it,
the sign in which we conquer.

**Suffering Lord,
your love for me is boundless.
Help me to learn that my hurts
may become for me the path to peace –
a peace that the world cannot give.
Amen.**

7 JESUS FALLS FOR THE FIRST TIME

"Exhausted he collapses, still clinging awkwardly to the cross that has fallen on top of him."

Sr Mary Stephen CRSS

Looking at that tortured hand
one wonders simply at the pain,
not just the physical torment
but the spiritual anguish, "that double agony".

Torture has its different dimensions –
pain … distress … torment … anguish …

It is made more acute by the wickedness of the perpetrator,
by "man's inhumanity to man"

Suffering often seems meaningless, or even evil –
natural disaster – which strangely we call an "Act of God" –
and the "thousand natural ills that flesh is heir to".
There are no real answers,
>   like children we can only put ourselves in God' hands,
>   for he is our mother and our father,
> >   confident that "All manner of things shall be well".
Perhaps knowing that such suffering is shared,
can give new strength ... resilience ... hope.

There are occasions too when we suffer because of sin –
>   our own ... or others' ...
This is harder to bear,
because like our first parents
barred from the Garden of Eden,
we are forced to face the problem of evil –
to which we find no easy answers.

Here is a plea that is also a prayer.
It was inspired by the evidence of torture camps.
It suggests that against all expectations,
compassion and forgiveness may indeed reign
in the bleakest of places –
like finding roses in the wilderness.

Cry wrenched wrung wounded radiant hearts,
"O Christ forgive!"
Beg nailed gnarled bloodied Christened hands,
"Dear Jesu, bless!"
Smile blind burnt sunken glowing eyes,
"Have mercy, Lord!"
Plead toiled torn aching tempered frames,
"Sweet Master, save!"

"In his weak and exhausted state all he can do is to put out
his hand towards his Mother.
Her response is to take his hand in both of hers.
No words are necessary.
Their love passes through their hands."

Sr Mary Stephen CRSS

What tenderness is in this meeting,
>	and compassion – a suffering with.
It is indeed wordless,
>	for no words can convey the depth of feeling –
>	sadness … anger …
>	hurt … fear …
So this mutual gesture speaks simply of love.

Mary promises –
>	comfort … consolation … strength …

Her Son is saying to her –
>	"Mother!" … "Hold me!" …
>	"Stay with me in my need!" …
Thus may children speak to their parents today.

"Look and see if there is any sorrow like my sorrow
which the Lord inflicted on the day of his fierce anger."

Lamentations 1:12

The prophet speaks of the Suffering Servant of God
who will take the sins of the world on his shoulders.
"O generous love that he who smote
In man for man the foe"   *John Henry Newman*
It seems a contradiction,
but it may lead us to discover something of the meaning
>	of mercy … of compassion … of hope.

Lord, be merciful to me a sinner!
I pray for forgiveness,
consolation and strength;
that I may learn to be, like you,
full of compassion and hope.
Amen.

9 SIMON OF CYRENE SHARES THE BURDEN

"Near to falling again, Simon comes to his rescue and takes some of the weight of the cross.
He may not have been given any choice about this but it became a great blessing for him."

Sr Mary Stephen CRSS

Who was Simon?
    at least we know where he came from.
Why was he there?
    As pilgrim to Jerusalem? ...
    to visit family or friends? ... to see the sights? ...

It must have been a day that changed his life –
pressganged into helping a condemned man
carry the cross on which he was to be nailed –
for all he knew just a common criminal.

He shared the burden,
and in that sharing, found
    not affliction, but blessing …
    not humiliation, but consecration.
Perhaps he had an inkling that
    a cross may bring new life …
    a life without end, for ever.

There is much for me to learn in this –
    that my hand, is a gift for others …
    that friendship is given as it is received …
    that the demands and rewards of friendship
      are without limit.

Here is that wonderful prayer attributed to St Francis:

Lord, make me an instrument of your peace:
Where there is hatred, let me sow love;
where there is injury, let me sow pardon;
where there is doubt, let me sow faith;
where there is despair, let me give hope;
where there is darkness, let me give light;
where there is sadness, let me give joy.

O Divine Master, grant that I may seek
not to be comforted, but to comfort;
not to be understood, but to understand;
not to be loved, but to love.
For it is in giving that we receive,
in forgiving that we are forgiven,
and in dying that we are born to eternal life.

"Veronica chooses to fight her way through soldiers and rabble to offer what comfort she can. She wipes away some of the blood, spittle and sweat from his face."

Sr Mary Stephen CRSS

She is nameless until this moment,
one of the unknown, silent disciples,
whose only wish is to be present.
Now she is named and known for all time
by her simple gesture, as – kind ...compassionate ...gentle
...courageous ...known by a true act of love.

Her reward, unasked for but instant,
    is to be given a name which means
    "True Image"... "*Vera Icon*".
That she is unknown in the gospels is no matter;
    she stands for all those
    who care selflessly for others.
Their reward is like hers,
    they carry the face of Christ,
    and show a truly Christlike image.

Remember those selfless servants,
    who give without counting the cost ...
    who weep for those whose tears are smothered ...
    who tend the wounds of the hurt ...
    who bind up hearts that are broken ...
    who touch the untouchable ...

Let today's Veronicas be my model.

As God's chosen ones, holy and beloved,
clothe yourselves with
compassion, kindness, humility,
meekness, and patience.
Bear with one anther and,
if anyone has a complaint against another,
forgive each other;
just as the Lord has forgiven you,
so you also must forgive.
Above all, clothe yourselves with love,
which binds everything together in perfect harmony.
And let the peace of Christ rule in your hearts,
to which indeed you were called in the one body.

Colossians 3:12-15

11 JESUS FALLS A SECOND TIME

"In spite of some help from Simon, Jesus falls yet again, trying to save himself with his hand spread out as he meets the ground. The yellow background might suggest sandy ground but the yellow can also express the sharpness of jarring pain. All this under the dark weight of the cross."

Sr Mary Stephen CRSS

Nothing can prevent this shattering fall as he
    stumbles and lurches on the uneven road.
His outstretched hand
    becomes the focus
    of a new pain that washes over him,
    jarring ... throbbing ... cascading ...
The agony is ...
    dark – bleak, threatening, yet shadowy ...
    all pervading – he is racked, in total anguish ...

May I see this as a parable
for the sinner to ponder?
Not to make excuses,
but so that I may learn that
my encumbrances may be the paths to sin:
my obsession for –
    comfort and wealth ...
the distractions that –
    prevent clear sight and blur reality ...
the friendships that –
    exclude, rather than embrace ...
    distract, rather than focus ...
This may be the haze that obscures God's presence to me
and cause my many stumbles
on my own uneven road.

But come what may I must never despair.

**May the God of our Lord Jesus Christ,
the Father of glory,
enlighten the eyes of your mind,
so that you can see what hope
his call holds for you,
what rich glories
he has promised the saints will inherit. Amen.**

Ephesians 1:17-18

"Jesus meets a group of women weeping and lamenting over the disaster that is happening to him. He tells them to weep for themselves. Far worse things are coming. 'For if men will use the green wood (him) like this, what will happen when it is dry?', when it is separated from his life. Hence the green around his hand held out in a tender comforting gesture."

Sr Mary Stephen CRSS

Who were these women who risked
the soldiers and the crowds to reach out to Jesus?
Just ordinary people who perhaps –
    had known him ... listened to him ...
    been fed by him ... been healed by him ...
And now they comforted him
    by their presence and by their tears.

Compassion means to "suffer with",
    not sentiment, but a deep sharing ...
    not pity, but a profound sympathy ...
    not just sadness, but a reaching out ...
It is practical, unselfish and mutually enriching.

The presence of these women is a precious gift to Jesus –
    support in an hour of need ...
    a sign of friendship ... a real presence ...

Their tears soften his agony ... a drop in the sea of pain,
yet infinitely worthwhile ... a pledge of comfort.
These ordinary women were great in their humanity.
We are all singled out for greatness –
"chosen before creation began" ...
chosen for our unknown future ...
chosen for God's companionship.

**You did not choose me,
no, I chose you;
and I commissioned you
to go out and bear fruit**
John 15:11
**From birth we carry within ourselves,
the seeds of personal growth.
Each of us can bear the fruit
proposed for us by God.**
From Pope Paul VI This is Progress

13 JESUS FALLS YET AGAIN

"Jesus falls a third time. He is nearly there but he has reached the limit of his strength. He collapses flat on his face entangled with the cross.
The purples and reds, colours of suffering and pain are growing as he/we come nearer to Calvary – the place of execution."

Sr Mary Stephen CRSS

It seems he can go no further ...
he has reached a threshold – the perimeter of endurance ...
      the brink of total collapse ... the edge of desolation ...
Can even now he hear his Father's voice
"This is my Son, my beloved" – or is he close to despair?
It will not be long before we hear him cry,
"My God, my God, why have you forsaken me?"   *Mark 15:34*

We're all caught up with his suffering –
     "And if we are children, then we are heirs,
     heirs of God and joint heirs with Christ,
     provided that we share his suffering,
     so as to share his glory."   *Romans 8:17*

We're all caught up with his cross –
marked with the cross at baptism ... signed with the cross
at our prayers ...sharing in the cross in our daily life ...
our faith is built on the cross.

Isaiah wrote of the Suffering Servant

**Like a sapling he grew up before him,
like a root in arid ground.
He had no form or charm to attract us,
no beauty to win our hearts;
he was despised, the lowest of men,
a man of sorrows, familiar with suffering,
one from whom, as it were, we averted our gaze,
despised, for whom we had no regard.
Yet ours were the sufferings he was bearing,
ours the sorrows he was carrying,
while we thought of him as someone being punished
and struck with affliction by God;
whereas he was being wounded for our rebellions,
crushed because of our guilt;
the punishment reconciling us fell on him,
and we have been healed by his bruises.**

Isaiah 53:2-5

"He has arrived. Now his clothes are stripped from him. By this time they must have stuck to his scourged body and bleeding back, so the process will not only have been humiliating but excruciatingly painful. I hope the roughness with which it is done comes across in the painting."

Sr Mary Stephen CRSS

Here, at Golgotha, the "place of the skull",
the one who is Lord
accepts the limitations of being a man,
    "like us in all things but sin".
He truly knows –
    humiliation ... degradation ...
    shame ... as his clothes are ripped from him.
He truly experiences pain –
    tearing ... screaming ... shuddering ...
        through his torn and lacerated body.
St Paul, troubled by a "thorn in the flesh",
three times pleads with the Lord to be freed ...
but the Lord tells him:
    My grace is sufficient for you,
    for my power is made perfect in weakness.
Paul responds:
    I will all the more gladly boast of my weaknesses,
    that the power of Christ may rest upon me.

2 Corinthians 12:9

To know my frailty is –
    the beginning of my healing ...
    a step towards wholeness ...
    a dying to falsehood ...

Let the same mind be in you that was in Christ Jesus,
who, though he was in the form of God,
did not regard equality with God
as something to be exploited,
but emptied himself,
taking the form of a slave,
being born in human likeness.
And being found in human form,
he humbled himself
and became obedient to the point of death –
even death on a cross.

Philippians 2:5-8

15 JESUS IS NAILED TO THE CROSS

"The lines and colours in the background are intended to express writhing in pain and the force of the hammer blows as the nails are driven through his wrist. Darkness is closing in on him."

Sr Mary Stephen CRSS

The hammer blows
drive the nails
through living flesh –
    cramped ... twisted ...
    taut ... locked ...

Pain grips him in its vice –
    floods ...
    suffuses ...
    envelopes ...
his whole being,
and locks his limbs.

Hands and nails embrace each other –
    warped ...
    twisted ...
    racked ...
"The gnarls of the nails in thee."   *Gerard Manly Hopkins*

Mankind is expert at such barbarism –
    genocide ... torture ... child abuse ...
    murder ... rape ...

Mankind is also practised in humanity –
    forgiveness ... care ... kindness ...
    gentleness ... sympathy ...

**Come down and prove yourself
they cry,
but the nails of love do not yield.
Upon those
who are nailed to life
and hang reluctantly
against its rough grain,
look kindly compassionate Lord.**

Kevin Nichols

16 JESUS IS CRUCIFIED

"The climax is reached.
The full intensity of the pain is expressed in the power of
the red background as well as the contorted hand."

Sr Mary Stephen CRSS

THE SEVEN WORDS OF JESUS FROM THE CROSS

He hangs on the cross for three hours –
tortured by cramp and thirst ...pain washes over him
... he drifts in and out of consciousness ... and speaks –

"Father, forgive them, for they know not what they do."   Luke 23:34
He begs forgiveness for his executioners ...
thus may we pray for any who harm us ...
Forgiveness is divine.

"Truly I say to you, today you will be with me in paradise."   Luke 23:43
A promise of salvation for one of those executed with him –
every sinner can take heart from this ...
repentance assures salvation.

"Woman behold your son; son behold your mother."   John 19:26
He speaks to his mother Mary, and to the apostle John
commending each to the other ...
mutual respect promises lifetime care ...

"My God, my God, why have you forsaken me?"   Mark:15:34
That awesome cry wrenched from Jesus
in the depth of his agony ...
The cry of all who feel abandoned –
by those who love them ...

"I thirst"   John 19:28
Death approaches ...
May what I thirst for,
prepare me for my dying.

"It is finished"   John 19:30
All you gave me to do
is done ... accomplished ... completed ...

"Father, into your hands I commit my spirit!"   Luke 23:46
Amen ... AMEN ... AMEN

"The pain is now over – still plenty of suffering for all his friends, but for him it is over. His hand, being held by Mary, is lifeless. The red has gone but the purple of suffering and sorrow predominates."

Sr Mary Stephen CRSS

Limp ... lifeless ... dead –
      spark of life fled ... warmth of presence chilled ...
      breath of being stilled ...

There is no more –
      pain ... joy ...
      excitement ... anticipation ...

Time ended ... heart arrested ... eyes vacant –
      not tranquillity but emptiness ...
      not peace but nothingness ...
            no more presence ...

For family and friends, all is changed –
the climax of death,
      dulls hope ... blurs vision ...
      sharpens remembrance ...
What expectations can there now be?
      None?

All that can be done is to
      pay reverence to this poor, battered body,
            empty ...
            lifeless ...
The hope of resurrection
      is itself in shadow ... stifled
I can hold the body well,
      respectfully ... gently ...
      tenderly ... lovingly ...

**At death
there are no more tomorrows
only a memory of yesterdays
and an eternal present
safe in God's hands.**

"The burial cloth is laid over his body and he is at peace. Very little purple remains."

Sr Mary Stephen CRSS

Peace ...
    not an absence of past –
        strife ... noise ... hurt ... emotion ...
    but the welling up of a new –
        stillness ... silence ... healing ...rest ...
All is calm.

Those still faithful to him still care for him –
wrap his mangled body in a sheet ...
drape his torn head with a cloth ...
close his tomb ...

His followers for the most part flee, moved by –
sadness ... sorrow ... shame ...
dread for the future ...

Those who killed him drift away ...
dissatisfied, unsure, confused ...
setting a guard on his sealed tomb ...
for fear he would be stolen ...

All is silent ... still ... hushed ...
Is there expectancy in the air? ...
Is there still hope? ...
And after death? ...
New birth? ...

Lord, Lord, do you hear me?
Lord, show me my door,
take me by the hand.
Open the door,
show me the way,
the path leading to joy, to light.
Michel Quoist

I am the resurrection and the life.
Those who believe in me,
even though they die, will live,
and everyone who lives and believes in me
will never die.
John 11:25-26

19 ON THE THIRD DAY JESUS ROSE FROM THE DEAD

"All is now glory and light. To demonstrate that it is really him he shows them his hands and asks them to touch him and feel that he is no ghost or vision. His new transformed life has begun."

Sr Mary Stephen CRSS

"Look at my hands and my feet; yes, it is I indeed."

Luke 24:39/40

All is new ...
all manner of things shall be new ...
the wounded hands and side
      are become agents –
         of hope ... of life ... of excitement ...
God, that tremendous lover, is on my side –
      ... nothing can destroy me
      ... nothing can come between me
        and the love of God
        made visible in Christ Jesus our risen Lord.

He fulfils my hope –
      his forgiveness breeds hope ...
      his love nurtures hope ...
      his compassion confirms hope ...

Do not be anxious about many things ...
      captive to fear ...
      worried about tomorrow ...
      restless in your responsibilities ...

Jesus Christ is risen from the dead, and brings –
      a new spring to our living ...
      a new expectancy to our vision ...
      a new depth to our faith ...

Love lives again, that with the dead has been;
Love is come again, like wheat that springeth green.
J.M.C Crum

Christ when he died
Deceived the cross
And on death's side
Threw all the loss.
The captive world awaked and found
The prisoner loose, the jailer bound.
Richard Crashaw

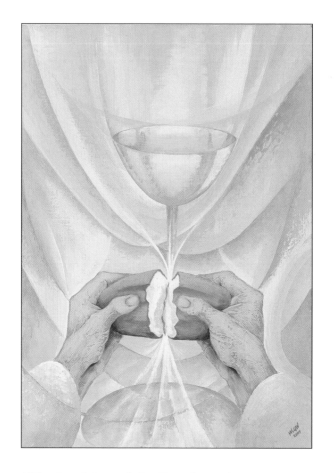

"The breaking of the Bread continues. Emmaus, the Mass, Christ in heaven and for all eternity. God suffers still – the bread is being broken still – but it is also continually being transformed into light."

Sr Mary Stephen CRSS

Bread broken ... Wine poured out ...
   for salvation –
      of all people ... of all peoples ...
      in all times and seasons ...
      in every corner of God's world ...

The Risen Christ is –
   Passover ...   *1 Corinthians 5:7*
     Cornerstone ...   *Psalm 118:22*
       Dayspring ...   *Luke 1:78*
   Good Shepherd ...   *John 10:11*
     Bread of Life ...   *John 6:32*
       Light of the World ...   *John 8:12*
Mediator ...   *1 Timothy 2:5*
   Head of the Church ...   *Ephesians 1:22*
     The Resurrection and the Life ...   *John 11:25*

The Risen Christ desires our –
   friendship ... communion ... faithful companionship ...
that we may become today's –
   apostles ... evangelists ... saints ...

We are ambassadors for Christ,
   through whom God appeals –   *2 Corinthians 5:20*
   ... we needs must pray.

**Who seeks to pray must first abandon life
acknowledging the sovereign source of good
that holds secure the world and all its strife
redeemed and saved by beckoning arms on wood.
In loss of self we find th'eternal One
enfolding us in urgent, pulsing breath.
So each becomes a living soul, new won
to be at one with him who conquered death.
Now quickened by God's Spirit we can speak
as friend to friend in intimate appeal.
This Presence found, no more is there to seek;
forgiveness reaped, no more is there to heal.
Be still, absorbed, held safe in God's own hand,
at peace with all who throng his welcoming land.**